CREATION'S SYMPHONY

My Writings to God

God Bless you!

Tim Stewart

Timothy D. Stewart

Creation's Symphony
My Writings to God
by Timothy D. Stewart

Printed in the United States of America

ISBN 978-1-60647-770-0

www.xulonpress.com

ACKNOWLEDGMENTS

To the encouragers of my life:
Lord, I love You and thank You for teaching me to laugh and for helping me to see the laughter in life. I don't know of anything better you could have taught me.

To my friends, Michael and Sid: your friendships have helped me to grow and have left a lasting impact on me.

To my brother Toby, his wife Kim and my nephews Caleb, Noah & Zach: I love you all. Thank you for always believing in me and teaching me how to have fun and, most importantly, for teaching me how to "rock out." Here's to further "rock out" sessions.

To my sister Sarah: Thanks for fueling my creativity by being a wonderful listener to my ramblings and always making me remember who I am, illness or not. And to your hubbie, George, for continuing the "spider hands."

To my Aunt Lauri: thank you for being a great aunt and for always reminding me to write. Here's to hard work, I think?

To Mom and Pops: You both are wonderful Christians who inspire me. Thank you Pops for making me smile again. My writing "Song of My Heart" says it all. Mom, your selflessness is an example. You know all you have done. Thank you.

This book would have never happened if it wasn't for all of you. I love you all.

The above individuals are not the only encouragers in my life. Thanks to everyone who has encouraged and inspired me over the years. This book is for all of you.

CONTENTS

Drawings of God

Who am I that You have taken time to sketch in my storybook?
Your creation is a symphony
a tapestry of beautiful artwork
a mighty woodwork
a beautiful melody of spring colors
a vase of red and white roses
the colors of my heart

Author of creation
artist of faith
love changer

Poetic words to a Father
a love letter dear God
my prayer to a beautiful King

I see Your framework of creation
the melody of sounds
the orchestra
serving
loving
hoping this beautiful array gets seen
an artist's scrapbook

Lord, I am stuck in a butterfly gaze whose timeless beauty
skillfully and craftily caused a surrendering of my heart

What I wanted to say is my joy is singing with Your creation
the melody of birds whisper Your name
in Your sketch book
Your scrapbook
my storybook
You write to me
I find You in me
You sketch
You paint colors of a heart in grace

Where My Eye Meets You

Oh tender heart
oh merciful King
love unfolds
love never fails
the clouds rise to just above the mountains
where my eye meets You

The vapor is still
the story unfolds on top of those mountains
it tells of valleys and peaks
oh the beauty of the Carolina mountains

A rush of life
and there's a glimpse of who You want me to be
morning slumber turning into a joyful day
my pride has gotten the best of me
but, today's a new day
bright and hopefully fulfilling

You're in the mystery of that smoke
You make trails on my heart
God of wonder
God of the ages
Your story is on top of those mountains
where my eyes meet You
and my heart thumps and thumps louder

Beautiful golden silence
beautiful loving Savior
beautiful day
beautiful day

A Canary

Telling stories isn't my thing
but I have a story worth telling
of regret and guilt
of pain
even hurt
that found themselves
in the hands of a singer

See, that's what He is to me
in my dreams
but I had to stop
to look within myself
and stop lying

He met with the wanderings
in my life
and sung to my soul
a canary
whispering sweet grace
in my ears

Beautiful Fear

Beautiful saving love I capture and write to You
loving me
changing me into the person I want to be
dreams are on my mind
and the reckless selfish abandonment I have lived

Rule my selfish pride
take it from me
I write to Thee God with God-shaped ink
forging new ways to praise my God
tackle me
turn me
twist my selfish pride into worthy love to You

Savior's rock, I cry
gathering stones, I throw no more
my reckless passion knows no bounds
yet deep in the ocean depths of my heart
You write on those tablets in ink of red
I write to You today, free and worthy
set in stone by You
so I write to You in hope that my words find You

Beautifully awakened
beautifully lost
beautiful grace powers down rocks
the tunes of this song are for You
tackling my fears
reshaping my heart as we speak

Travel on my heart
step
press down
compress love on my heart in the wilderness
I cry like others before You
refusing your love
refusing to let you reshape my heart

So carefully and beautifully change me
mold me like Thee on this fine Sunday morning

The Silent Cheer

A silent voice is heard in the morning
just write, I say, of the morning mist at dawn
a bird in flight spreads its wings
they gather together and get in their raft
just write, I say, of beautiful rushing waters
the light spills out from the clouds moving apart
their voices gently get louder
a trout jumps
beautiful roses in spring time
moss gathers on rocks
the sun is rising
a flash is brilliant

One Christian squints his eyes as he tries to clear his throat
the universe is so vast
so bright
rise today in me, Lord
"Beautiful is on the horizon," a Christian friend shouts
they gather for prayer and recognize that creation whispers of a
lovely God
just write, I say, of God's love on that sunny, bright day
"Let's start our ride," exclaims the leader
so they start down the canyon

The river walls capture their hearts as they ride by
all the quiet they've ever known rings out so true
so small
I am so small, they all think
the gentle wind captures nature's love
swooping birds are caught in nature's circle on the horizon

Just write, I say, and I think of the Lord
I am surrendering all I know
friends gathering together splashing fun at each other
just write, I say, for those beautiful rushing waters
I must admit I am lost in the wonder of Your silence
just write of this group of Christians on the way to their destination

A silent rain starts
gentle drops suddenly get harder
the wind begins to swirl and it hurls this group down the rushing
rapids
the leader's awe turns to concern
they huddle together
yes, I say, they huddle together
they begin to pray for their deliverer to get them to safety

Suddenly, they realize they are in for the ride of their lives
the wildness and fury of the river
turns into freedom for those in the raft
gathering their thoughts
letting loose
for they know that their Savior has them in the midst of a tight grip
I am so small, they think, but so important to the Lord
"He numbers our hairs," one Christian shouts
just write, I say, of the canyons echo
just write, I say, of this band of brothers
just write, I say, of our Savior

Just write of this morning as the morning mist evaporates
into a beautiful gaze upon the slippery rocks
just write I say of those beautiful, rushing waters
just write and I think of You, Lord
I am surrendering all I know
just write, I say, and I think of the Lord
I am surrendering all I know
friends gathering together, splashing fun at each other
just write, I say, for those beautiful rushing waters
I must admit I am lost in the wonder of Your silence
just write of this group of Christians on the way to their destination

I must admit I am lost in Your silence
I must admit I love You
I must admit I love You

A Christmas Prayer

Lord, all I can do is bring myself
bring the pain
the suffering
my tears and my cries
help me to be a servant this Christmas
help me to be a witness
to help people in need
and to see Your birth fresh and anew

Help me to grow into the man You want to see
help grow my heart and grow me closer to You, Jesus
help me to be myself and cry with those that are suffering

I'm nothing without You
You're the miracle worker
change me
move in me
get me on my knees and have a servant's heart
let me be humble
let me cry
and let me be lowly in spirit
You are so good Lord!

You humbled Yourself to the cross
my cries You heard
You are forever faithful
help me to open my feelings to other people
help me produce
to be quiet in heart
You use ordinary people
I'm ordinary

Work in me Lord
again bring tears to my eyes
bring joy to my life
bring friends and family
open my eyes
help me to get on my knees
and have a servant's heart

The King of Hearts

Here it is, a story of romance, of the heart between one kid and an old man and a deck of cards. Now, as the story goes, the old man noticed his card hand and noticed the four of a kind that had gotten him down the river so many times - see they were on a boat. As the deck of the boat got more slippery, the river began to flow quieter and quieter and the life giving beautifulness of grace, flowed over the edge of the boat onto their feet. The current rose and the wind naturally blew and the older "poker" of a fellow found it in himself to search for the King of Hearts.

I say to you so, the old man looks at his cards and again sees the dreaded four of a kind, the dreaded four eights. The man searched in his heart as much as he could. In purity of mind the kid lay down His cards. "I've got a four, five, seven, nine and an ace," said the kid.

The old man looked at his cards, he had four eights and the king of hearts. Now at this time, as the story goes, the four eight's were blown from the old man's hand by the growing wind. The old man cried uncontrollably.

"Kid, I've got the king of hearts." The old man had lost. Is the story over? No, here's the great part. The kid smiled and watched as the river waves crashed up onto the rocks. The kid winks. The old man looked down at the king of hearts in his hand and it is said that the old man never won another game in his life. Except for that day, somehow his heart of hearts was aced by a reckless wind. See the boy had aced his life and the old man finally understood that it was all right to lose with the King of Hearts and win the game of his life.

The blessed King of Kings doesn't play games with the hearts of His children. The King of Kings saved that old man's soul the day that old man decided to accept grace and search in his heart for the one true Savior - accept Jesus Christ today.

Diary

These tears
these fears
these scars
these prayers
the cross Lord brings me to my knees tonight
hoping in my tears that this love letter finds its way to Your heart
tonight
see I can't wait any longer
I can't take much more
I need You tonight
I need Your brilliant skies
that awesome thunder and that blazing lightning
to open my heart like years ago
like when I first found You

Dear Lord it's been years
years wandering aimlessly in this burning wilderness
storm by storm
storms they came
bringing me down many times
yet stronger and closer I grow to You
stronger and closer
I don't know what to write anymore, just to write
just to write of those fireflies that lit up my heart's light
those huge snowdrifts that kept me in wonder
those stars that kept my head held high
sparkling, sending dreams my way

Dear Lord, it's been minutes since I felt You
too long I guess
long and bending like a river's journey
if it's a journey of the heart, I want it to be Your heart I find
growing closer to Your hands holding mine
I've written You before
a galaxy of tears
dear Savior, You gave Your life for me
You have certainly taken this heart for a ride
when it's all said and done, I don't know if I could go through it
again

Lord shape my heart strings
shape my heart
shape this song
shape this diary for You

Growing

Stormy seas shake me at the thought of You
and sharing my thoughts couldn't be harder
but I have come to the point where something must be done
and something must be shared

See, I am so scared
I am so worried
but the Lord pushes me on
to step beyond
preparing me
He guides me
settling here to my destination

So I just write what comes to my mind
Why me, Lord?
Why this pain?
Why this hurt?
but you gather me at this point
rescuing my heart
rescuing me in the blowing wind

Trusting
turning to You
tackling my fears
so I write
write to You
throwing off my mask
throwing all to the wind

Heart of this Land

There's freedom in an eagles flight
fury in a blowing snow storm
wildness in a star thrown across the sky
God's sights and sounds are on the wind
restless in the hearts of a holy nation
there's something at the heart of this land
that is rocked by thunder and lightning
and spilled on by rain

A mountain stream finds its way home to lower pastures
an ocean wave wildly thrown against the shore
a song singing at dawn where dew drops off leaves
and morning violins sing the rise of a hot Carolina sun

Someone who laid the foundation
who looks down from heaven with love
and sparkles at night
whose warmth can be felt by a fire

Someone who's looking down
guiding the twinkle in my eye
melting my heart
His footprints across the sky

Laughter in My Life

Lord, I can't wait to talk to You tonight
gliding in a circle on nature's horizon is a beautiful flock of birds
up in the air my soul is flying with them
it's been a while since I have seen a sunrise
to feel alive

My heart is in a beautiful mess
tossed and torn without You whispering in my ear
my thoughts turn to You, Father and Your loving grace

My heart is on fire
up in the air
I lift You up my Savior
for a minute
for a moment
a smile between us lasts a lifetime

There's something different today
so many clouds in my life are moving apart
I'm waking up with the laughter of a Savior
that brightens up the sky

Beautiful and brilliant horizons
are calling out to me
Your laughter is spilling over into my life
so I walk in the light of Your love
laughter in my life

It Means Something

Lord, I lay down my pen
there are some thing's that cannot be written
but I pick up my pen again
I did something special yesterday
Lord, it's got to mean something
all this striving to get through something
what do we have to measure our love but reaching our goals
tiredly
exhaustedly
but doing it Lord

Lord, it's got to mean something
Why do I tell people about this?
Lord, is it something you throw at us for our enjoyment?
I'm not one for enjoyment
I want to strive in writing this
it's who I am

I pick up my pen again
to say I did something special again
and I won't let it get away from me
You can live in the special
Lord, this has got to mean something
all the writings
all the heart, all the mind, all the soul and all the strength

Lord, thank You for this
Can I put my love for You in words?
there is so much more ... much more ... more

Well, here you go Lord
I am on Your heels Lord and this song can't take that away
so Lord I pick up my pen again
to say so much hard work has to pay off
Lord, I love You
thank You wonderful Savior
something sweet and special
and then You pick up my pen
it's all about the suffering
it's loving You with all the heart, all the mind, all the soul and all the strength
yes Lord, it means something

Assurance

My reasons and doubts have cast a shadow on my life
only to realize my dreams are not so far away with Jesus
looking forever until I see
I now look to You, Lord, for guidance
and I look towards the future
to a future bright

So many pious actions
deeper convictions I need
wrestling with so much
anxiousness calming down
and I am with You and You are with me
looking forever until I see
Lord, create in me a pure heart
create in me a steadfast heart
my prayer is to overcome
to wrestle no more

Lord, quiet the anxiety within me, although I'll wait
cast my burdens aside, only if I come to You
settle me down and let me rest in Your grace
and see that I am not perfect and am surely in need of a Savior
and I rest in that knowledge
oh Lord let me rest in that knowledge

Dream

The sun set in my heart tonight
setting, where inside all is calm
and rain then poured down thoughts of peace
and I am learning to walk with my Savior
and learning to lay down and rest
for my heart is oceans away
in far away lands
where I can discover, act on, and pour out my faith

So the sun set in my heart
pouring down thoughts of peace
raining down thoughts of grace

The time is now
to reach out to a lost and crying world
a hungry lost world in search of a Savior
He's reaching out to you
Christ wants to be in your life
He won't give up on you

So the sun rose in my heart
the day my heart was swept away
growing older ... searching
I found the only thing worth pursuing is life lived with grace
life lived with a Savior

The Leaf of My Life

Time speaks of bright tight melodies of love
red roses and beautifully colored leaves
change can be good, and is good for a heart that needs it

Sometimes I think I travel at the speed of light
but what I want is for that light to flash bright red and orange
the changing of the seasons, the changing of my soul

Music shifts now to a new beat
a beat of wonder and amazement and, yes, grace
so what I want people to know is that I love the Lord
and He loves me

Tight, bright melodies play to leaves shaking free from the trees
and sparkling their way down to the ground
my gaze is upward on You
You're changing colors and bright Mondays

I am learning, Lord, that Your love never changes
not like those leaves
it has been there all along
carried me in fact to better places
to shifting sand and back

To tomorrow I say sing this song of introspection
insight into the Lord's changing style
You rock me, Lord
You change me
You make me into something sweet
You make me feel like that leaf

Beautiful Deep Blue

The skies are beautiful tonight
the horizon is pretty
a deep blue
the setting sun and birds ignite my soul
I see the ocean in Your eyes
to Your beauty, Jesus
roses in spring time

So here's to originality
love, poetry, conversation and skies
create in me art
words to say
to a beautiful, shining King
I know you're so wonderful
the skies proclaim Your work

Just writing of Your love
You're the beautiful deep ocean
in spring time a field of wild flowers
a child dances in them
You're a sudden, burning blaze of the dawn
simple and sweet
lovely work
sudden rush of love
sudden rush of roses
Lord look, a smile
there's a smile on the horizon
it's me Lord
Your beautiful creation is singing Your name
and there are words between us
I love You Jesus
I love You Jesus
I love You Jesus

Grandma

As I search inside myself to get the feelings out
I search inside for the beauty that lies within her
I see the beauty of red roses
red violets
and the sky just before dawn
the beauty erupts like a volcano bursting its force
yet hot and calm
and the beauty speaks of ages

The beauty is like the rising of the sun
the red shooting particles lighting up the sky all at once
it's a beauty that lasts
that speaks a lifetime of love and kind words to a grandson

Your beauty outlasts us all and speaks of the generations that look
up to you
just look up at the stars
their beauty speaks brightness and fun
that's what you are to me, Grandma

I Need to be Me

The walls have come crashing down
my pride has been swallowed up by a moment with a Savior
my eyes are opened to a world that needs me to be me, with no
mask

I need to be me, I need to be me

Lord, I give You my tears
I give You my heart and my shadows
I give You my voice
to help others find You
because You whisper to me in prayer

I need to be me
I need to be me
I need to help You

You opened the door of my heart
and are helping me form tears of how I treated You badly
You're giving me a voice inside to cry out in the night
I am fine right now
You kept me forming the words of this song

I don't need much to help You
I need me to be me
just me, being me
I need to be me
I need to be me

Swaying flowers in a field below stars and storms in the sky
a lit up cross
sparkling sentiments on a Colorado mountain side

I need to be me
I need to be me

Give Me Reasons

Lord, my goal is far from You
let me return and make my path straight
give me reasons to write
give me truth to erase this aching in my heart
settle my thoughts around Your might
give me words to say Lord
give me the right attitude of heart
give me reasons to have fun
develop a man inside
work me through my fears
come by my side Father
show our relationship
give me wings to spread
give me reasons to say I love You
I know, I don't need any more reasons
Father, I come to You
not with all the answers
but that's alright
the rivers right in You

Ocean Run

Wow! words through an ocean run
I put on my favorite song and pick up the pace
bus stops are on my mind
looking for something different
something new
Tim, who are you?

The ocean hits me and knocks me over
I'm not searching for perfection in my heart
grace again tackles me like one of the waves
a movie stays close to my heart
I hurry so I can finish this song before my dad gets home

The excitement of a new day hits me
grace comes with the tears of the ocean as I run by
and I don't care for once
and I write to the ocean
you're one of God's greatest creations
look at all the fish

My mind comes on all the fish in the sea
and I think, Is there one for me?
and the rhythm of a writer chimes in
and grace pours out like the kid dumping sand on my feet
and I think - this run, thank You Lord
Who am I?
I am more than this run, now that's pretty good

Broken Beauty

Lord, I get so frustrated
this pain speaks volumes
snowy days are still in my dreams
without You though they are nothing

The star shoots across the sky
my heart shoots with it
somehow and somewhere
these words sting so deep

But what about right now?
every sentence means so much
but I am crying on the inside
is this love?
is this pain?

Just let me think before I write
let it spring from the heart
I am broken, I admit it
the shadows have come
don't let the smiles cease
broken beauty
but it's me

So Tall - Nephews

To have and hold you
to reach out to give you a hug
to see you lift your brow
to see you dance
to see you smile
to see you grow and sprout up,
like a strong tree with good roots
to see you enjoy the day
and run, your heart on fire

Your growing legs
built tough and strong
growing tall
built like a mighty fortress
good and tall
so I look, and smile
to see you grow right in front of me

Burning Horizon

Toby, there goes an eagle soaring overhead
its wind stirring up sentiments inside
and all its beauty and strength lifts up my soul
and I know the Lord has something more for us

Toby, there goes a hawk bursting into flight
fast and gliding, circling on nature's horizon
and I am thinking
all that beauty
all that motion deep within

All that my song can say
is that there's love on the way
a future bright for a Savior's son

The music bright and fulfilling
those cold Colorado foothills
they're burning bright in flight
as we take sight of our goal

That wind sets our sails
pushes our souls on
sets our spirits ablaze
our love in motion

So much to say
so many songs I wanted you to hear
so I put pen to paper, a rush of ink
to tell of my love for you

God's Love Left Standing

I have seen You with me
next to a quiet river in winter
when all inside seemed lifeless

I have seen You in the countless hours of writing
when all seemed hopeless
yet somehow what is left standing is a man

When all that is left is a man's courage to continue
it's a lesson I had to wait to learn
when all I can imagine is adversity calling me to something better
life seems so challenging
so joyless

When nothing is left, but to struggle
and all that is left is to hope
it's a lesson learned over time
for the future is more than happiness
and life comes with sorrow
as sobering as Your love is
it's a love worth finding

Shattered

My world is opened
crushed and broken
bruised and battered
but my heart is Yours,
though shattered and torn

There's a fire inside
burning bright for You
inside, spilling outward
fresh and fulfilling

Moving apart
the clouds separate
the heavy storm moves away

You're a breath away
You hear my sighing
and answer my prayers
by healing this heart

Broken open is my life
my destiny revealed
a life and eternity
meant with You

Shadows are removed
songs are introduced
puddles are missed
as warmth fills my life

You meet me with whispers
in songs and with light
with a brilliant song overhead
as moon and stars shine

Continuing to guide
whispering
my heart is filled

Grace

Lord, I only feel at home when I am writing, creating, but somehow the words don't always come out right. Ironic, don't you think? When listening to some of my favorite music I feel inspired. I just want to create, to share, to stumble with words. The beauty of the horizon lights a smile. A sudden hush, an intimate talk and here we are Lord. Suddenly grace awakens me and I am at a loss for words. Timidity gives way to creation, birds sing and I skid across the pavement like a tumbling leaf.

What do I have to say that is different and who am I to serve? Yes Lord, Your beauty has caused my heart to still and I breathe for once. I breathe in, and to be honest, You already know my reaction. The breath was everything I could have dreamed for and more. Lord, I know what to say. I love You. But I don't know how this is going to end and that is joyful. Spring is coming. The day is coming. Am I prepared? Will I do it right? I must admit that is what I am thinking. However, You calm me, settle me and somehow change me again from the inside of this apartment. I must admit the walls of this place calm me. These things I have learned Lord, I enjoy walks, sorrow is a part of life and breakfast is a good start to the day. What I am really trying to say is that You're the most honest, good, genuine person I have met. So fiddle me Lord, play me a tune. Grace's melody is playing creation's symphony. Somehow I manage to get a few more words in, a few more chances to say sorry because it feels good. Honestly prepare me Lord.

God, I must admit I am a sinner and I come to You. Poetry fills my head as music plays and dreams are forever set in that moment. I must admit the view outside my apartment is breathtaking, the trees towering, the bird's nest nestled in the corner of our deck roof. Everything's so quiet, so still. Yet still, small songs can be heard chirping the morning through. Songs of hope, rest and love. Songs that grace, God's gift, can only play. The melody is heard far off yet so near to my heart. I just write and talk of our Savior's moment, His whole life in fact. Who am I to serve such a God?

So words fill the day through, sunshine splits the morning horizon in two, as I squint to get a picture, a view of God on high. The sunrise dances and plays music, sweet music all the day through - that of fiddles and violins. So I pick up and produce art or produce songs in my head and hope to play once again for You Lord. I don't know how to play but somewhere in the shiny moment of the sun glaring down on me I can hear that song - the stone rolled away, creation's singing it. I hear it call.

Okay Lord, what do I do with my time? Paint You a picture with a thousand words, describe the silence that causes an aching in my heart, sing causing a rise in my spirits, make melody with the maker of time, or just write, write of love on the darkest night, cry out with words too deep to express or watch the moon's shine sing?

The stars declare Your wonder. I must say Your beauty outlasts me, takes me to places I have never been. I must say this aching for You grows, grows every time I hear nature silent, every time I spend time with a loving mother. Conversation, dear God, with You is what I long for, deep intimate talks of the past, present, and future. Moment by moment I am learning, learning dear God that time keeps on moving, that love is best serving, that hope keeps me alive, that suddenly You're there. Suddenly, there's a smile and I think of You, Your brilliant displays, Your handiwork, Your color scheme, Your God drawings, Your molding, Your love and I think what do I have to do with it? I must admit I think tears of joy are coming with the clouds.

Have you ever seen a brilliant display of wild flowers, or a garden of love between friends? Have you ever wished time didn't go so fast or taken time to worship, truly worship? Have you ever wanted something so bad you think that you found it? Well, I must admit You've done it all, Lord, shaped the moon, walked the streets, played with children, rescued me ... what's next Lord? Maybe I just enjoy, enjoy words that paint a thousand pictures and sing praises to my God.

It Would be Called Love

The song I wish I could write would come right now
I wouldn't have to pretend
it would push my imagination but not too much
it would possess beauty
talk of my sinful pride
cleanse me
talk of You, Jesus, and honestly speak to me
through it all it would give me a sense of wonder and love

Most of all the words would be there
the process would give way to freedom
I would call
You would listen
forgive me would come to mind
my love would speak of You

The song I would write would meet my expectations
it would be never ending
it would tell me how much I care about Jesus
it wouldn't be the perfect song
it would be me with my imperfections

I wouldn't give up
I wouldn't give up
I wouldn't give up
but most of all it would speak of You Jesus
Your love
a sinner, I come

Beautiful King

The music comes on
and my thoughts are stirred
by emotions and feelings about an act of salvation
which brings tears of joy
I'm brought into something wonderful
sorrowful pain changes me
changes me

so sweet
so sweet
forever the wind so still
right and wrong
direction
compass
what shirt to wear
wind
everything changes me
changes me

Splashing in Puddles

As I pause to lift up praises
to a holy God raining down blessings

Splashing in the puddles
my eyes fix toward heaven
You say, just write Tim

So I write my best
to a lovely God
I see Your framework of creation
Your God drawings
Your beautiful flowers

I take a glance upward
splashing in these puddles

The Ocean Inside

Wintering the storm inside
the sunshine soothes my spirit
my aching turns into gladness
soaring, my spirit flies to You
settling my thoughts
giving me direction
the compass of my heart
a star's timeless beauty
gives way to grace

You can't be that good
but You are
You can't give us that
but You did

Lord, You bring me a smile
give wings to my flightless heart
You're the chill in the air that catches my breath
the moon's bright glow
calm me
settle me

Praise Song

I am singing inside
the melody inside sings out
I love You Lord
You create inside
stars sprinkled across the sky
as I hum the words to You
the melody crashes against the shore
this love is Yours Lord
higher than I sing
but the beauty of the mountains
pushes and sets this heart afire

I love You Lord
You create inside
stars sprinkled across the sky
as I hum the words to You

This new song I sing
You're more than enough
the tide rises in the reflecting moon
and I will sing

I love You Lord
You create inside
stars sprinkled across the sky
as I hum the words to You

I want to praise You today, Lord
Your flowers in the field are splendor to the eye
I love You, Lord
so I write to You
as I listen to beautiful music and sing inside my soul

What am I singing but praises to my King
I love You
only I ask Lord, give me the words to praise You Lord
with a melody inside
so inspired
quench this thirst
I love You, my King
higher than the heavens is Your glory
on my walk
the rose petals sing
stars sprinkled across the sky

Flight

Whisper silently tonight
whisper gently Lord
release my flightless heart
erase this aching
give me wings to spread

Soaring high
sweeping in the deep blue sky
over the rumbling ocean
over the white sandy soil, the Siesta sand
the still towering trees

You give me flight
through the red Carolina sunbeams
I notice the angles of branches
a mathematician's dream
bursting into flight
rising with the tide my spirit soars
sweeping
swooping
settling on the ground
my destination, this room with You, Jesus
my friend

I Will Wait

I will wait Lord
for my fears to dissolve in Your love
along with my questions dissolving in Your substance

I will wait
for my false interpretations
of You and our relationship
to dissolve in Your truth

I will wait
To get on my knees and ask for Your forgiveness

I will wait
for I know day by day You will sustain me
and I will rest in Your grace
I will wait for that to happen

I will wait on You Lord
for my questions to dissolve
and to look ahead
so I put my fears aside
and set aside my failures
You have forgiven them

Writing

There's something that whispers in the dark
that is sturdy and still as an oak
it's my compass
giving me directions through the night
connecting those moments of grace and beauty
that tells me You're there Lord
somehow sending
lending its hand
connecting the story of my salvation

It gets me up in the morning
and lays me down at night
relinquishing my fears
helping the tears come forward
so I just write and write and write
in the still of a quiet morning, I write

The Music Inside

A song, a poem you sing from your soul
capturing the hearts of those who will listen
a poem of stars and galaxies, light and love

A song that follows flapping wings and shooting stars
whose melody rises and falls
a brother's gentle laughter
a sister's gliding dance

Jesus, Your music touches my heart
setting me free to love out loud
Your soul's song is bold and breathtaking
gentle as a summer's rain

Jesus, Your soul's song
carries me to where mountains rush the sky
floats me down rivers of delight
sends me soaring strong

Blazing Summer

Lord, I am at a loss for words
this haunting past blazing in my memory again
and I am struggling again to express
how much You love me

Driving across open fields lit up by lightning
that bright hot summer that shook me to the core
it still haunts
changing me still

There is so much I want to say to You now
about that blue Colorado sky and bright nights
about love, our time together, and my heart

Some days now, the sun seems to be too bright
and some days it's hard to get around
the beautiful storms that have lit up my life

It still haunts
beautifully haunts

Cheerful Song

Nephews, brothers, sisters, mothers, fathers
your voices are beautiful
this is my song tonight
and in my heart I cry for You, Jesus
to sweep me up in Your will
to settle me here tonight

My heart is crying inside for You
slowly aching, burning for You
this is my cheerful song tonight

Nephews, brothers, sisters, mothers, fathers
your voices are beautiful
this is my song tonight

The flowers are blooming
and I am climbing the mountains
the lakes and trees are still and quiet
and I hear your voices
this is my song tonight
my cheerful song
this, my cheerful song tonight

My Sandals

Short and sweet
gorgeous fun on Sunday morn
melodies of fruits and leaves storm the branches of my heart
rocks beneath my feet
walking, not running on shifting sand

Shinny bright red and orange leaves
quiet … awe … inspiring
sandals of time
looking, changing, making, moving, lasting
soothing to a crying heart

A walk so bright
orchestrating my spirit
gorgeous fun on Sunday morn
my lasting impression, God cries out to me
laughing, smiling, changing the colors of my heart

To me dear God
my heart, my love, my times
awaken me to fall's sweet smelling aroma
a mindset
a colorful change
a mockingbird, a hummingbird
organized thoughts
what to do?

The sunrise, not the sunset of my spirit-filled soul
cries out to turn the page of thought
my heart, my love
my King, my Jesus
my hope
my everything's sweet smell

Conversations in season
the season of change
to bright and better days
to the future untold yet set in stone
the stones beneath my feet
time stands still yet moves underneath my sandals
my sandals
my sandals, my sandals ...

Ready to Sail

There's music in Your words, Lord
there's a style to Your rhymes
I won't get far without You Lord

There's a song worth dancing to
words worth hearing, not because they're mine

There's a reason to write tonight
a reason not to give-up
Lord, give me a reason
Why should I expect anything more?

There's a reason to write tonight
there's so much dancing on the inside
I want to sail the open seas
breathe in the deep blue sky
for there is a reason to write
it is for others to read by the lamp light
so don't tackle me with Your waves, Lord
give me peace to sail through the storm.

Music lifts my soul
give wings to my heart
burn inside me Lord
reach inside and pull out a man

So inspired, there's a reason to write
so I gather all that's inside and hit the open waves

Prayer Song

Lord, so much to say
but how?
give me reasons to write
I can give You my heart
it's going to take some time
time, to let You rise in my spirit
and send the rest crashing down
so give me patience
and open this prayer
it's what I need
because You are what I need

Give the words for the next line
let me rest in You
and just write to You
a love letter from the heart
soaring high
may I bathe in Your peace
I know You need to hear me
and are waiting patiently
let me patiently wait for You

So I raise the white flag
and I come to You
I come to You, Father
to say I love You
to say I'll wait
to say I'll wait

The sky is getting ready to erupt
I am looking up at the stars
just sitting by a quiet river
looking at those snow-capped mountains
and realizing, Jesus
I will fight for You

So let me wait
let me wait
let me wait

Honesty of Heart

So much hidden worrisome thoughts
my shadows become puddles of light
so many instances away from You
but my questions are dissolved in You
take away the doubt, regrets and blame
let the river rush my shame away
further I will go, up the mountain
and through the valleys in my life

Erase these fears, Holy Father
settle this aching and give me peace Lord
further I will go up the mountains and
through the valleys in my life

Take away these oceans of tears that I lay at Your feet
rescue me Lord away from the filth
Master, guide me
let my thoughts dwell on what is noble and pure
What am I trying to say?
I want to be closer to You, Jesus
I want time to dissolve this hurt

Beautiful Story

I love You with all my heart, all my mind,
all my soul, and all my strength
it's snowing out so I have some time to write
now I am different
not looking out the blinds at life anymore
I have become that picture
never giving up
now I have something to write
but I always had something to write

I have a story to write
now a beautiful one
I knew it would always be
Isn't life great?
Lord, don't stop me now
I give up to You Lord
and there You are
and there I am
fighting for my life
never giving up
that's how I want it

Lord, I just wanted to say hi in my struggling
Lord, that's me
struggling
Lord, that's You
You and I attached to each other's leg
I love You Lord
I will do it Lord
Lord, all my love for You

Jesus Lead Me On

Let me push through the storm
and settle here beneath the sky
not just to watch those sunsets and sunrises
but to come to know You – to know You more

I will learn in love
somehow You find me tonight
I will let Your spirit lead me on through my life
into the light of Your love
Jesus, lead me on
the wind lifts me up through the storms
further down the road

Clearing Skies

What I really needed was You
afternoon skies are clearing
blowing away the dust
so all that remains
is pain being removed by beauty

Puddles and shadows
removed by warmth and light
clouds breaking open
by rays of sunshine

A sky breathing all His delights
blue, full, and wide
music in the sky
settling my thoughts

Savior, my sky is wide open
my heart is changing
what can I say, so inspired
so thankful for this smile

Then, why can't I say what I mean?
Why do I feel so broken?
Why can't I fall on my knees and cry tears of love?

All that we've been through
leads me through hard times
all that cries out with the past
I'm moving on
I'm cutting loose
the wounds of love
cutting ties to the past

So thankful for knowing the Savior of the world
so thankful for these tears
so thankful for You, Jesus

The Story of My Heart

Oh, there's music inside
and it resides in the deep quiet part of my heart
where the Lord resides
in the deep blue reservoir I call home

So I write notes and parts
for You and I to whisper to each other
and for me to call out
I am learning that each day is new in Your grace
in Your will

So I write parts with a quiet anticipation
a heart gone quiet
by the silent cold of winter
where stillness reigns
I can imagine what's next for me
I am learning that the fears I had are vanishing
quick, like seeing your breath in the cold air
and I am settling
here in my home
quietly sitting
enjoying
Lord, the love You have

God's Voice

As a child full of faith and fire
catching snow flurries in my mouth
I understand now
I can hear Your voice
through dust blown winds
and storm driven nights

It's untarnished and open
like a wild horse bucking and unbroken
I hear it next to quiet rivers and mighty oceans

It changes, forcing action
like mighty gale force winds
it's strong and sturdy
moving past like a freight train
full of steam and power

It's bright
like a glimpse of that South Carolina sun
gladdening the heart
like finally landing a trout
to a constantly seeking fisherman

It changes
shaking us to the very core
loud like stampeding elephants
quiet like the sounds of summer

A Sunny Day

Sometimes it comes along
the beauty – all it's cracked up to be
words are enough and You are there
Your sweet sound
Your silent sound
Your whispering
the orchestra in my mind
the colors of my heart
where my eye meets You

Your light - the shine through the blinds hits my eye
my soul is restored
I see Your warmth
Your protecting
and I cry out, Abba Father!
I cry out to You
the light sound of music vibrates my heart
my wants
through the glare You say hi

River Wild

My questions dissolve in You
I may never know the answers
but I know there's hope
a light at the end of the tunnel
where beauty flows like a river rushing
waterfalls fall into mighty pools

Summers on my mind
and the dead of heat in the middle of the day
gives way to a relaxing cool night
where storms are blown away by your gentleness
I am shaken, still standing tall
I am oceans away from You Lord
oceans away from where I need to be
but my anxieties and worries dissolve
like falling raindrops
washing me to where words flow
and I need to be
all of these flowing thoughts
and I am forever taught to be more like You

Summer's on the way
and I look at it favorably
because Your music flies inside of me
lighting up the night like a well lit firefly
and I look to see that You're there
and You are

So Your process gives way to Your freedom
and Your light can be seen miles away
a familiar song comes on
and I am reminded of past things
all we've held and let go, shaping our future
so I just write of the river wild and Your gentle wind
how it relaxes, changes and Your guide leads on
through the mountains, valleys, oceans and away

So I press on through the spring into summer
and write to You one last line on the river wild

Tim's Rock Song

Skies and stars
brilliant stars and skies
I'm back writing
setting down lyrics
to honor Your majesty Lord
to honor a beautiful King
to ask for love, poetry and roses in spring time

I have never had more fun
never could create like You Lord
song for song Your glory prevails

Love songs to Jesus is what I want to write
my love letter to that deep blue ocean
lovely works
Your creation is singing Lord
beautiful rainbows
mighty rivers
I look to see that You're there and You are

So here's my ode to music
to the songs that have lifted my soul
to the songs Your church has made
the skies proclaim Your work
Your rushing waters reveal Your love
Your mountains capture my eyes
Your love in the spring time lighting my life
Your direction is clear
Your originality is beautiful
my love song to You will make its way to Your ears
lovely Father
love, poetry and roses in spring time

Life's Sorrow

Lord, I want to grow deeper spiritually
I want this soul to know You more
quiet music plays in my ears
suddenly, I am found in Your arms
and You won't let go
You won't let go
you reach in and grow this heart deeper

So I write in the still of night
and search for You longer
I am looking to grow up Lord
looking for spiritual maturity
looking for a Savior to wipe these tears away

You are there to teach me
to correct me
to mature me
to help me learn that with life comes sorrow
Jesus you died for me
You cried so I could see what a man should be

So music stop
quiet break through to my heart
quiet storm, You leave me breathless for more

My Symphony

Thunder rocks and rolls
ocean waves crash on shore
stars sprinkled across the sky
and I feel good tonight
a symphony plays

Violins in the morning
dew at dawn
blowing mist gathers
and hits my face
and suddenly I smile this morning

Rivers run
kites fly
kids play
stories are told
and a Savior's smiles
for how His son has turned out

Gazing at the sky
a flight of thunderous birds
a horizon blazing red at dawn
the height and depth the music reaches
it finds me in a simple grin
so I fly
I fly away with the music
the stars
and a symphony of Jesus Christ's love for me

Pursuit

I wanted that awesome song tonight
I wanted a fun song
I write a song that has to be has to be these things
but I have found out that it's not what you write, it's the pursuit
a smile creeps in
I ask the Lord to make me enjoy something for once
but I know it's more than that
I find enjoyment creeping in again

I write with all my heart, all my mind, all my soul
and all my strength ... and it's more
Lord, with Your grace
the battle is already won
I smile
cry for fun
leap for excitement
maybe dance for You Lord once again
and I work hard
I work harder for happiness
it's in those times you don't feel like doing anything
that you push yourself anyways
I choose you Lord
fighting a similar battle again
but then it's the pursuit, isn't it?
and happiness creeps in again

I write with all my heart, all my mind, all my soul, all my strength
Lord, because of Your grace,
I sing praises to You
I laugh at adversity and sing with beauty
rain comes down and I cry to my family
a river of happiness and proud success
enjoying a right relationship with the Lord

let me work enough
let it be enough
so it's not the beautiful words I use
it's the constant pursuit
the constant push
it's that striving
it's writing
it's pursuing

I write with all my heart, all my mind, all my soul
all my strength ... and it's more
and it's more
Lord, because of Your grace,
I will write You a story
a beautiful one
my confidence grows
it's that push

I have spunk, Lord spunk for You
I jump in with both feet
I love You Lord and I smile and think this is new
I love my life and I find words worth writing
and my fears about what to write subside
as I put my love for You in words
it gets quiet now
You and me Lord, without music
just give me something special Lord, something new
please Lord, maybe a night of writing
I would say Your name and smile
it's the striving
let my work be enough
one more time isn't going to kill me Lord

I love You with all my heart, all my mind,
all my soul, all my strength
Lord, because of Your grace,
I will give You a song
a smile creeps in and stays awhile
and again I put into words Your beautiful love
and say God, I love You
words spring into life, how much You must love me
I know I am going to make it and beat this thing
but it's more
it's then I realize, grace
You gave that to me on the cross

Friends

Through storm shaken skies
raining down rivers of doubt,
the sun pushes through
valleys turn to mountain tops
where friends talk
there is music and butterflies
and songs in the light
a Savior's gentle wind pushes them forward
He's their all
and His love calls out to them

Later in life I sing songs from my heart
with love and light and a pen in my hand
and form the words that mean the most to me, I love You Jesus
and through the blowing wind and the tough climb
and blurry snow I have seen You
You have broken my heart open to a world in need
it's about You Jesus, my best friend

Song about Dad

Dad, there was music inside I wanted you to hear
lyrics I hadn't finished
letters I wanted to compose
poetry I wanted to recite
love songs, Dad, I wanted to sing
big dreams I wanted to share

I saw our Savior in a field of wildflowers
in a barefoot beach walk
up in the angle of branches
in a moist snowflake

Mountain streams I wanted to fish
snowballs I wanted to throw
conversations about lightning and wind
I wanted to tell you in a field of swaying flowers
Daddy, I have become an artist

See Daddy all I know is to lift my head to Him
and say, Savior, I'm all here
and all I know is that blazing sun sets the sky on fire
and those burning Colorado hills
will be forever in my dreams
and those stars
those stars, they're twinkling

So here I am Daddy
lifting my words to heaven
where a Savior still sits at the right hand of God
and the fog rises early in the morning
and I can see clearly
that God is working in my life

So in a distance between smiles
and galaxies below where I should be
a Savior's joy finds little old me
and distant mountains and jumping trout, Daddy
will forever remind me of you

And every time I write a song
or make a child laugh
or climb higher than I ever thought
I will be reminded of your bearded smile
See Daddy, nothing moves me like a song
all I know is I can't wait to see my Savior
and in heaven with a song on my lips
I will be practicing
I just wanted to say, Daddy, I love you too

(Tim's father passed away in 2005)

Roomies

Upside down cake
popcorn
smiling inside
opening up the blinds
the Lord has given us another day
fun
love is enough
smile
birds fly outside

Beautiful heart
beautiful mind
beautiful heart
beautiful mind

The swaying wind won't get us
The sound of coming storm clouds, do you hear?
we have protection
a roof above our heads
a resting place
an exciting place
the river merges into one
grace will be our shield
our fun
our soothing memories
the Lord will be our guide
our freedom
our love

Sequels and Sand

Lost and gone, if for a moment
the littlest wave knocking me over
burned out and broken
so steep and staggering
I make my way in the night
in the light of the moon

I'm dreaming of You again
thoughts pouring forth by the ocean
moist sand making its way beneath my toes

Scatter brain
moving Your way Lord
push me on
settling here
standing
still standing
if for a moment the gentle wave
can knock me down
but Your laughter keeps me up

My eyes make it toward You
releasing the smile of my life
playing with You on the inside

If for a moment the moon's bright glow
seems to be reaching out
someday, somewhere, some steps down this road
I will grow like You want me to
while spinning tales on the far horizon

Creation Song

Butterflies flutter before me
as I reach out to get a touch
and that's when my questions dissolve
and my fears subside
it's like when I was nestled on a rock beside a quiet river
where the love in my life rang out
and You silenced my heart
where I could bear tears
and saw the man You were making me in to
it's the same when I gaze up into those stars
when memories are made in my family
it's when life seems so good

You're the maker of that light
it's in those moments
I know there's a love wider than I can comprehend
I love You Lord
writer of my songs
deeper than I can see or imagine or can love

So I write to tell stories
how You have taken me to new places
silent places where I've never been
so, moment by moment I am trusting You more
trusting that You will shape me right, Father
so quiet inside, ring out so true
Lord, You're what it's all about
let's go deeper, further, further Lord
teach me Your way
so I look to You Lord
and write for You some more

Journey of Faith

"Come on Tim," put one foot in front of the other
on this journey of faith
this love walk
on this poem of life

You allow me to be myself
what a great gift
I had to grow up
I had to experience sorrow
it's okay to say sorrow
You died for me
adversity comes
You suffered and died
but I must walk on

"Come on Tim," put one foot in front of the other
on this ocean of waves and worries
so I just write
life takes some time to get used to
Is what I'm saying worth saying?

A Savior's Beauty

Beautiful Savior, open this letter
a rush of ink for You
my heart is searching for the Author of Creation again
so I write to my Savior
I write a love letter, dear God
to speak of the deep blue we all look up at
to speak of red roses and bright Mondays
I am searching again for the King of Hearts
in the hand I was given
it's a card we all get
if we take the time to notice the beauty of the moment

So I write to open the creativity in my heart
I think it worked
beautiful Granny, beautiful Mom
love letter, dear God
art
looking
searching
hoping to find all I have asked for and dreamed for
searching, in God forged ink, is a writer, dear God

There it is, the beauty of grace
all I have dreamed, asked and hoped for
where does the beauty lie?
in my searching?
in Your creation?
no, it lies in You, beautiful Savior
the beauty of grace lies in You
lives in You
beautiful Savior
lives in You

Your Hope Stills Me

The river flows quietly these days
the sound is refreshing, soothing
nothing beats the silence of God

The calmness, the hush, the gentle breeze
silently You whisper to me
soothing sounds to a boy in need

The violin is playing
the strings are beautiful
Your spirit, Your tenderness in silence
You are strong, God
the words don't seem to be there now
but You're there, the words will come
knock off this selfish pride
You are my silent hope
quietly refreshing me

Sweet and Funny Dance

Thank You Lord for this living mountain top
You've pushed me through the valley deeps
looking down the slope I let out a long sigh
remembering why

You have surrounded me with love
blessed me in so many ways
listening and learning
looking and laughing
I burst forth in song and dance

So long boy, hello man
so long valley, hello mountain top
so long hurt, hello character
so long, long, long trail - hello home

I have been smiling lately
quiet reflection never felt so good
awe is settling in
burning a bright fire
raining down thoughts of peace
listening and learning
looking and laughing
I burst forth in song and dance

Hello resting place
goodbye steep hill, hello breath
so long staggering, hello head lifted high
so long old tune, hello new song
so long, long, long sigh - hello smile

Lord, I'm going to stick to what You've taught me
I am going to hold fast to these lessons of life
listening and learning
looking and laughing
I burst forth in song and dance

So long loneliness, hello family and friends
so long heavy pack, hello arms held high
so long somberness, hello joy
so long worrying about what others think, hello Jesus
thank You for this living mountain top

Letter to God

So it's time to put the story together
I don't know what to say
I wish I had a lot to say tonight
I guess I am just wishing
wishing that my words will make it to Your heart
I guess I am just wishing for more

If it never happens
I will continue to write
to a lovely God
so I will wait
Is it too much to ask?
Is it too much to write?
I know this pen is failing You
it's then You speak
You say "Just keep writing
because this silence is for Me, not you"
So I write on

Song in My Heart

In my dreams
Colorado mountains are gleaming in the west
in their shadows
jumping trout and birds of the air
sing Your name Lord
for You are greatly to be praised

You and I, Pops, can be found in those streams
you with your black hat and fly rod
me looking on in wonder of the God who made the heavens
honor and majesty are before Him

I am singing a new song in my heart today
because of your generous spirit
and because I have found a father in you

Stars are sprinkling my heart
getting me ready
for the Lord is coming to judge the earth
I just wanted to say daddy, that I love you

The music of a son's heart
can be heard through his songs to his father
where his heart is echoed in the words he writes
it's never to late to say
I want to grow up to be like you

And my heart will sing your name to my Father in heaven

Boyish Dream

I know it's rising within me
a melody worth singing
a song worth telling
a song for You, Lord

A song of morning violins
of a boy dancing in a field
of wildflowers and a summer's buggish haze

He's crying out from deep within
telling the story of my heart
of love tied to a beautiful Father
so give me a reason to write
a reason to rhyme and not to give up
but to write one last line

The boy is me
the song that is sung is You
it's me dancing in Your fields
a boyish dream coming true
a song that has to be sung
from me to my Creator
of ocean waves and beach walks
and time with You

Those silent stars
those silent times
near rivers, lakes, looking at those mountains
still as a heartbeat
cold and alive
just listening
just listening to You
suddenly You're found
and the good things continue to come
and Your love continues to be there
a song worth writing
worth telling of You and me

Shaper of the Stars

Lord, You are the shaper of my songs and those stars
so if You're listening I hope You hear the truth
for the Lord is mighty and erases my falls
with Him I'll stand, if I am to stand at all

So take a look inside and hear the music calling
because Jesus, You have my emotions flowing
and all I have known before has come crashing down
because spending moments with You is everything

Let Jesus' warmth rush into your life
His mercy and grace are ever-flowing
for we all fall short of His glory
and the Glory of the Universe wants to rest in your heart

All I know is just to write
His beauty has transformed my life
and I find it is so natural
to lay it down before my Father

Thank You

Thank You Lord for this moment
thank You for this life and Your loving hand
deep in Your eyes I see warmth and laughter
changing my life
changing my life

Thank you for today Lord
thank You for the blue sky above me
rolling along I see my dreams in Your eyes too
Your love is spilling out
into my changing heart, loving me

Thank You Lord for my family
thank You Lord for my friends
I see You in their eyes
in the love that they send my way
Your heart is beautiful and broken
I will come to You Lord
and let Your heart change me

So I will step and step
and grow and change
as our relationship grows
and changes into the power
I find in Your eyes

You love me
change me
How can I not tell about You?
keep me growing Lord
thank You Lord, thank You

Your Gentle Whisper

The ocean tide is rising up to my ankles again
the moist sand soothing as I walk
in the light of the moon by the ocean
it's glow so startling, yet so soul refreshing
the moment passes slowly
introducing a familiar ache for You

I'm playing on the inside again
a young child
the gentle breeze against my face
forcing a forgotten smile
forcing action
releasing laughter and grace
if only this moment could last a lifetime
and I remember
Your promise of love for a lifetime
a promise to be with me always
sometimes it's too much to think
of how much You love me

Bird Flight

The sun blazing on fire
a bird in flight on the horizon
that brilliant golden sun
that high, deep blue ocean above
suddenly You get to me, Lord
suddenly that warmth, so shocking
I am lifted up tonight
with the birds in my mind

A rush of life from You
deep and wide You are
Your depths I don't know

Just writing what comes to my heart
that ocean inside, deep and wide
where your mercy flows
and that brilliant Carolina sun shines

You make trails on my heart
and set it on fire
ablaze by You
so much sentiment
bottled to fly
in that deep, blue sky with You

The Diary of My Heart is You Jesus

My hope is in Jesus Christ
the living hope of my resurrected heart
my love, the diary of my heart
my cry in the dark
my light
my song
my light
my future
my bright future

The diary of my heart is You Jesus
love birds sing the whisper of Your name
the songs of the lost
the salvation of us all
my memoir
my love
the search for the strength
the servant in us all
the troubled
the star in us all
the wings that take us in to flight

So I sing of You and find You tonight
in the unlikeness of someone like me
thank You Jesus
for the diary of my heart is You ...

Storms in the Sky

Lord, sweet violins play Your song so sweet
sweet as the blue sky above dust blown ground
long spreading wings in love drops of rain
rays of sunshine spreading hope

Art in branches
beauty in the birdbath
sketches in the clouds
music to the sound of passing squirrels
a world alive all around me

Beautiful rhythm in a passing soccer ball
volumes spoken through a hardworking parent
heights and depths to the laugh of a child
so much said in the storms around me

The sky erupting in the morning
leaves blown everywhere
all these beauties
inspiring
to reach heights I have never seen
and step into the unknown

Beautiful Silence

Quietly I whisper to You Lord
silently the silhouettes begin
tapestries so beautiful God
I love the ocean inside
somehow beautiful silence stills me
soon our love we find

Just write I say of the beautiful ocean waves
the silent water sips at my legs
the beauty is golden, the silence is vast
I find You tonight in the beauty of the siesta sand
somehow You tie the story in my heart together
somehow, oceans away, Your love finds me
the beautiful ocean, the calming hush
the beauty of silence … in the sand
at the beach I find You
humbly I approach You

I see the stars bright and inspiring
the moon dripping glow
the bird in the air
the breeze on my face
the chill of the night
caught in a moment
trusting You that I will do this right

Learning
finally growing up
the knots of love Christians tie together
soon I will wake to the beautiful sunrise
but for now I am lost in You
lost in Your beauty
in Your silence
and I just write
to say I love You on this quiet night

Stargazer

Lord, let this song flow through the fingertips of a writer
to tell of the dance of stars sparkling
dazzling us on the ground
and the bursting flight of a hawk
in those cold, burning Colorado hills
the beautiful dance of that South Carolina sunrise
to the joy of just writing what comes to my heart
brilliant, boyish dreams are fulfilled on nights like these
where you stare up into that deep blue, yellowish haze

Teach me how to use my talents
in hopes of finding that peace in You Jesus
who created that, oh great lake of my heart
age to age Your story flows
through the valleys in the hearts of those who believe

Those violins and fiddles stir me
shake me to the very bone
help me to grow into Your shoes
help me to realize all You have done for me
oh music of my heart

With one last push of our Savior's love
just writing one for you, Sis

Loosening Up

Thank you Lord for this day and Your many blessings
You shine through the sun and the moon
and change me through Your swirling winds
You're fun and I am laughing
loosening up because You're at my side
we run this race seeking for Your breath
to breath in us life and to last longer
it lifts up and pushes us further down this road

So I bring my heart and my love
laughing
loosening up
lifting me high
soaring
settling here with my thoughts
thriving on every word You whisper
so I write with a steady pace
and look beyond my fears and doubts
yeah, yeah I'm reaching out

So I smile and look up
change my direction once again
on this painful winding road
that takes us to new places
to paths we must decide and take
so when the decision comes
I will laugh and loosen up
because You're fun and fun ...

The Sound of the Violin

Beautiful violins play the quiet in my heart
the beat is lowered now to reach full efficiency
the violin is brown, rustic
melody is of spring
of early life
of weathered storms and bright Mondays

To toast your creation Lord
beauty resides in the unlikeliness of someone like me
soothing sounds play from this violin
the wind is calmed
the storm turns to sun
the sunshine inside my heart
the melody that of a master
the music jumps, a sounding cricket at dawn

The early morning mist sprays my ankles
the field is wet in the early morn
and I know You're there
playing Your violin
like a master
to Your creation
I'm in Your hands now
shape
shaping the strings of my heart Lord

Lord, Bring a Smile to My Face

Oh sunshine of my heart
next to beautiful rushing waters I dream
Lord, put together this story of my heart
and bring a smile to my face
these still waters guide me
these still waters silence me
do not let me be afraid, Lord
because what's next is You with me in eternity
so I just write today
to say I love You
for all that troubles my mind
will melt away with the rising of spring
the rising of the sun, the dawn of a new day
this is freedom
this is love
this is my heart
this is why I write
Andrew's CD's in my walkman
dreams forever set in that moment
so I keep in line and march on
the march of winter brings a smile to my face

Moving Forward

You're stirring something inside, Lord
tossing my feelings
hope is alive inside
because You make me alive
so much to say
so little time
moving forward
thoughts for a King
settle me Lord
question me
make me whole
take me somewhere new
something exciting is forming
something worth saying
moment by moment
glance by glance
we're settling down
to friendly smiles
warm handshakes
and real conversations

The Honesty Song

Honestly, somewhere I got lost
I'm old enough to admit it
Your faith is moving mountains
I'm scared of who I have become
and scared of who You are making me to be
somewhere in between I am lost in Your peace
lost enough to know You're shaping this very heart
lost enough to know Your wind is picking me up again
moving me to greener pastures
and beside still waters
lost enough to smile, lost in You

Honestly, I know I can go deeper, be deeper
and to know there's so much growing up to do
there's grace to admit that
I'm scared of who You are Lord
and scared of where this song is going
but somehow You keep this pen going
keep this body moving
keep this love of Yours growing inside
I am lost enough to know that

Lost enough to see the beauty in Your lakes
creative enough to share
grown up enough to know immaturity when I see it
and honest enough to know I've hurt You
but saved enough to know I am forgiven if I ask
so honesty saves the day
saves this day
and pushes this pen, ever flowing

Faithful Friend

To Jesus my friend
my faithful friend
through the morning sunrise I see Your beautiful face
the sun dances across the land
though the night shakes us
I look to see You there and You are
morning violins are playing Your tune
creation is singing Your symphony
music truer and louder than I can write

The sunshine wakes me today, a day above all other days
where I look and find that You've been fighting for me all along
though I fear, I will walk through the valleys
Your music shining and carrying me through
through the tunnels and through the storm I will go

So I just write of Your morning sunshine on my face
warmth so bright and fulfilling
God let me write to You

The sunrise dances fondly across the land
the music soft and inspiring, full and lovely
Savior, You have kept me in Your arms
Your hand is grasping mine
just writing of Your love towards us
brilliant, bright fun

So I gather all I can
and write a love song for You, Jesus
my faithful friend who has kept by my side
through thick and thin
and thicker ....

CPSIA information can be obtained at www.ICGtesting.com
Printed in the USA
LVOW06s1000300715

448155LV00002B/99/P